MODERN METHODS OF VOCATIONAL AND INDUSTRIAL TRAINING

Adebayo Ojo, B.Eng, R.Eng

MODERN METHODS OF VOCATIONAL AND INDUSTRIAL TRAINING

iUniverse books may be ordered through booksellers or by contacting:

iUniverse
1663 Liberty Drive
Bloomington, IN 47403
www.iuniverse.com
844-349-9409

ISBN: 978-1-6632-0268-0 (sc)
ISBN: 978-1-6632-0267-3 (e)

Library of Congress Control Number: 2020912255

Print information available on the last page.

iUniverse rev. date: 08/14/2020

CONTENTS

INTRODUCTION

Advancements in science and technology have reduced labor and increased production in many aspects of human endeavor.

As much as this can boost the economy of the manufacturing sector and services industries, the means of production—especially raw materials, labor, and capital—cannot be completely eliminated. Rather, better means of utilizing those means of production are in order.

Paramount is the labor factor. Entrepreneurs must be able to successfully run a business, and that means sourcing skilled labor. The need for skilled workers who can use modern tools efficiently—and, thus, for vocational and technical training—is more important now than ever.

This book focuses on reducing the time needed to train qualified employees without compromising quality. *Modern Methods of Vocational and Industrial Training* is a handbook for vocational and technical instructors and also industrial training officers. It covers the A to Z of skills acquisition, including planning and building training workshops.

1

PLANNING FOR TECHNICAL TRAINING

The Fundamental Aspects of Planning

Effective training is the result of careful planning. First, you'll need to make these fundamental decisions:

1. *What types of courses will be available.* Will the department train operators, trade apprentices, or technicians? Or will only retraining programs be offered?
2. *Where the courses will be held.* Find out what facilities are available for training and decide which is best suited, bearing in mind classroom size, workshop size, equipment needed, and location of the training department and staff.
3. *How many trainees will be enrolled per class.* This will depend on the available facilities.
4. *How long the courses will be.* The length of each course will be guided by its aim. For example, a retraining program may not be as long as a fresh training program, and an operator's course may not be as long as an apprentice course.
5. *Who will attend the training.* Training officers should have knowledge beforehand about trainees. Information such as age, sex, education level, health conditions, and, in some cases, height will help to determine the starting point of instruction.

Course Planning

The next step is constructing a course to suit the needs of the trainees. An instructional plan may have administrative and supervisory ramifications. Basically, it will consist of the following components:

1. Curriculums
2. Program of Studies
3. Course of Studies

Curriculums

A curriculum details the offering of a training establishment. It includes all the activities of the training department, both related to training and extracurricular activities (if any) outside the establishment.

Keeping a record of training department curriculums is a good idea for administrative purposes.

Program of Study

In its broadest sense, a program of studies is an orderly arrangement of the integrated subjects, activities, and experiences trainees will pursue in order to attain a specific goal. Respectively, learning involves the acquisition of knowledge, mastery of certain skills, and the development of desirable attitudes. The program of studies generally extends over a definitive period of time and is usually designed for certain groups of trainees.

For example, a two-year machine shop program of studies might include

- first year—with a division of terms, specifying the subjects to be covered and operations to be included in the duration of each, and
- second year—as tabulated in the first year.

Course of Study

A course of study is a comprehensive plan that shows the scope and teaching sequence of all the activities provided for a particular subject in a program of study. In short, it is the syllabus.

A course of study may consist of a mere outline of topics to be covered or processes to be performed. In complete form, it will include additional features for the purpose of assisting the training officers in the presentation of the subject matter.

One should be made for all subjects in a program of studies. For subjects requiring acquisition of both practical skills and knowledge, both should be laid out; that is, the course of study should include both operations involved and information required for the mastery of the skill and should be arranged in a way that will fit the trainees' needs.

Much will be achieved in course planning if the needs of the trainees are clear in our minds.

2

SKILLS ANALYSIS TRAINING

Skills analysis training is concerned with training for *work*. It enables people to produce goods and services in order to earn a living and is otherwise known as *vocational training*. It is essentially practical and utilitarian, as it involves doing things for a living.

To succeed, trainees must acquire the three essentials:

- skills
- knowledge
- the right attitude

When to Use Skills Analysis Training

Training for work in an industry demands well-planned and well-organized activity so that people can learn as quickly as possible. The decision whether to use skills analysis training must be basically economic. If it enables people to learn their jobs in less time and at less cost, use it. If not, don't.

Good training aims at, and is justified by, increased productivity (thus, the importance of not wasting time on learning).

Consider this rough guide on deciding whether to use skills analysis method:

1. If new workers can attain experienced workers standard (EWS) on the task in a week, explanation, demonstration, and safety and induction training will probably be adequate.
2. If new workers can attain EWS in one to three weeks, training within industry (TWI), preferably with targets and fault analysis training added, will usually suffice.
3. If new workers take three weeks or more to attain EWS, skills analysis training is likely to be the most economical method.

That said, there are situations in which it will be more economical even when learning times are shorter.

Why We Use Skills Analysis Training

The three main purposes of skills analysis training are

1. to enable new workers to attain the standards of output and quality of the experienced workers in the shortest possible time,
2. to retrain existing workers whose productivity or quality standards are below par, and
3. to train existing workers to undertake new and different types of work called for as a result of technological or market changes.

There are three principles that constitute the formation of industry training for skills at work:

1. The idea is to show the worker the job and leave him or her to pick up for him- or herself the standards of output and quality required.
2. The whole period up to the attainment of EWS of output and quality must be considered training.
3. An analysis and understanding of the skills and knowledge used by the experienced workers form the only satisfactory basis for training.

Three types of work are covered by the skills analysis approach:

1. *Semiskilled*—single-task job training
2. *Skilled*—multitasked craft apprenticeship training
3. *New work*—training for special tasks, a.k.a. postapprentice training

The important point to note here is that industrial training has to be considered on a task-to-task basis, whether the training be for skilled or for semiskilled work.

In general, applying skills analysis training reduces the time to attain EWS by about one-third.

How People Acquire Skills at Work

Movement is involved in acquiring skills, but movement is initiated by incoming information received by the five basic senses. There is also the sixth sense—the *kinesthetic sense*—which is the most important of the senses used in the acquisition of skills.

Kinesthetic sense is associated with the sense of touch, and it's the pressure we exert with our limbs. It also tells us the position we're in.

The importance of kinesthetic sense can be understood from the fact that people can live without sight, without hearing, without touch, or without taste, but it is virtually impossible for a human being to pursue an active life without the kinesthetic sense.

Our activities do not begin with movement but are initiated as a result of receiving sensory information. Incoming information, not the movement of any part of the body, constitutes the starting point of any performance. Thus, human performance depends on constantly receiving sensory information.

Human performance, then, results from two processes—first, the *receptor processes* (incoming sensory information from sight, touch, taste, and so on) and, second, the *effector processes* (those that concern the actual movement). These two sets of processes are interlinked and controlled by the brain, where the appropriate decisions are made.

The final result is that a skill is acquired only when a worker is able to control his or her movements much more precisely than an ordinary person.

How We Acquire Knowledge

The knowledge content of industrial tasks is not identical with what we acquire in a classroom situation.

The trainee who can write correct answers to examination questions about an industrial job is not necessarily the one who will be best able to perform it.

In industrial tasks, we need to acquire knowledge for practical purposes and for a response in action, not in words.

We have to use words and other symbols as a means of communication in all industrial training. And yet the learning of these symbols by themselves may contribute nothing to the skill of the task.

Therefore, modern industrial training has concentrated heavily on *activity methods*, as distinct from *verbal methods*, as limitations of the latter have become increasingly recognized.

Symbolic information is what we use for communication and retention of the knowledge content required in the performance of industrial tasks. To understand the relevant symbolic information, a prerequisite qualification is always necessary. Training tends to increase individual differences as the tasks increase in complexity.

3

INDUSTRIAL TRAINING

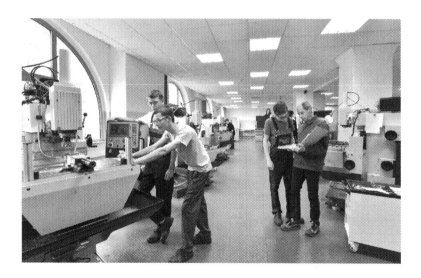

The history of training in industry may be traced back to the early days of apprenticeship—when our forebears had to spend several years training their children and relatives so they could occupy posts in the oldest industries—agriculture, hunting, fishing, and weaving.

Industrial training as we know it today is still in its infancy.

It will grow with our growing industrialization and technological development. It differs from its earlier form in two ways:

1. Modern training now includes induction training, or introductory courses designed to create a vital "sense of belonging" among new entrants into the industries.
2. The training periods necessary for producing skilled workers have been greatly shortened. This is because industrial training has been systematized.

Purpose

The purposes of training in industry are many. They include:

1. Helping workers to rapidly acquire skill
2. Boosting productivity and profitability
3. Improving the quality of workers' workmanship
4. Minimizing waste of materials and damage to tools, machines, and so on
5. Minimizing the need for constant supervision of people at work, net labor turnover, absenteeism, and unit costs of production
6. Helping workers to better utilize plants and machinery
7. Improving employee morale, versatility, and promotability
8. Revealing employees' potential and special talents

In order, therefore, to achieve and maintain these objectives, it is necessary to have well-controlled and continuous training programs and policies in every industry.

Industrial training (like any good teaching) depends, to a large extent, on the trainer's knowledge of the psychological aspects associated with learning. The psychological processes involved are

- conditioned response or habit formation (well treated by Ian Pavlov, a Russian psychologist);
- learning or practice curve and the cause of the "plateau";
- reactions to part and whole methods of presentation;
- transfer of dexterity or learning (See "How People Acquire Skills" in the previous chapter, as well as J. W. Cox's research findings on the subject);
- the involvement of the trainee's senses and emotions by the effective use of suitable teaching aids and procedures; and
- the arousal and length of trainees' attention (via the introduction of timely pauses and variety in what is being taught).

Training Needs

In determining a company's training needs, consideration must focus on

1. the skills and knowledge required at every level of the company's hierarchy, and
2. the strengths and weakness of its present workforce.

The relevant facts for the assessment of the requirements can be obtained from records of staff history and performances, job specifications and analyses, work-study techniques, and questioning and studying the subjects at works.

For instance, in the work-study approach, the comparison of an efficient worker's standards (in terms of times, quality, and quantity of the worker's output, and his or her skill if relevant) with the actual performances of jobholders will help highlight training needs.

There are various types of training in modern industries. An induction course varies in form and duration from industry to industry and from company to company within one industry. Craft apprenticeship, training for general work, demands the transfer of proficiency. Training for a specific job requires both theoretical and practical learning. Retraining or training of trained workers focuses on how to use improved methods or machines. Then there's training intended for supervisors and would-be trainers, skills analysis training, and management training. All these are other forms of industrial training.

A training scheme designed for prospective trainers usually has four main facets:

- job relations
- job methods
- job safety and accident prevention
- job instruction

A preplanned checklist—a sort of questionnaire—is distributed to the trainees as a basis for determining the progress of each trainee in turn.

Skills analysis training, on the other hand, is a combination of industrial psychology with the work-study method.

Methods

Employee training methods may be classified under five headings:

1. *Informational method.* This is the "pouring-in" or straight lecture method. It is ideal for a large group of inexperienced trainees.
2. *Instructional method.* This involves demonstration or a "learning-by-doing" method. It is effective if the group of trainees is small. Trainees must be guided, in any case, by a qualified instructor.
3. *Conference method.* This method involves the pooling of ideas by a group to solve their common task.

4. *Incidence method.* Using the incidence method, the instructor provides the skeleton (inadequate facts) and the trainees have to ask questions to make up the body of knowledge (the full particulars).

5. *Sensitivity, laboratory, or Bethel method.* This is the "uninstructed" or emotional involvement technique.

Today, the need for a training center or a vestibule school set aside as a part of the industry and equipped with training tools, such as blackboards, film strips, dummies, mockups, and the like, is imperative for companies whose labor force exceeds five hundred. Smaller companies may hire or borrow outside services or facilities from institutions like technology colleges, large training centers, and educational institutions offering short university courses. The United Nations Industrial Development Organization (UNIDO) is another resource.

Industrial training as a career requires practical teaching experience (not necessarily that of a lecturer) and some knowledge of the processes, techniques, and products of concern. It is an interesting career if it's punctuated with sufficient practical experience in the various functions of the unit sales, production, and work-study and other services—to lend color and confidence to the trainer's instructions. It is not a career that can be pursed in complete isolation. The trainer has to win the support of the management team and, if necessary, employ the services of outside trainers.

4

ANALYZING OPERATION FOR INSTRUCTIONAL PURPOSES

One of the distinguishing characteristics of technical training courses is that they provide experience involving manipulative work. The degree of skill to be mastered in performing this type of work depends considerably on the ends to be achieved.

Since manipulative work generally serves as the main basis of a course in technical training, it seems only logical that the first consideration, when planning a course, is the selection of what makes up the manipulative processes. The purpose of this chapter is to discuss the procedure for identifying the basic operations of a course.

For a good understanding of operation analysis, it's necessary to start by defining and discussing some common topics in technical training, which contribute to operation analysis. Among them are

1. occupation,
2. job, and
3. operation.

Occupation

This may be defined as that which occupies one's time in making a living. It's a phase in the field of employment. One's occupation contains skills to be mastered, knowledge to be acquired, and attitude to be learned.

Occupation Analysis

Analyzing an occupation has as its goal the development of a complete course of study for the purpose of teaching the occupation in its entirety.

There are many ways in which this can be done. Basically, all occupations involve certain manual skills and certain theoretical knowledge. Some of the things that apply to most occupations are listed below. The instructor can, however, add other materials that will make the analysis more comprehensive.

Components of most occupations include specific

1. jobs,
2. hand tools,
3. machinery,
4. equipment,
5. materials,
6. products and services, and
7. information (including related subjects).

From these aspects, operation analysis and related information will be sought out and related subjects planned.

To ease the problems of the analysis, the occupation will be divided into divisions or phases, either from the items listed above, or through the instructor's experience.

However, other sources may be of help to the instructor in the occupation analysis. These include

1. trade texts,
2. magazines,
3. newspapers,
4. handbooks,
5. manufacturers' catalogues,
6. industry literature,
7. service manuals,
8. job evaluation sheets,
9. government publications relating to the occupation, and
10. experienced specialists.

In the analysis, the occupation will be broken down into divisions; the divisions, broken down into subdivisions; and the jobs in each subdivision listed.

Occupation è Divisions è Subdivisionsè Jobs

Jobs

A job is a unit of the occupation consisting of a series of skills or operations utilized in the successful completion of the task. A job comprises different operations. Instructors do not teach the job but the skill.

Operation

An operation may be defined as a manipulative action performed while producing a finished article or a unit of work to be executed in repairing, preparing, replacing, installing, or adjusting any part of a fabricated product. The operation is the skill.

When production is involved, an article is manufactured, and the action being performed is called a *production operation*. As such, it is only one of a series of things that must be done to produce the article. Examples of this are drilling a hole or tapping a hole, skills performed in the production of a jig. Machinist and carpentry trades are a few occupations in which these types of operations are performed.

An action that repairs, replaces, cleans, prepares, installs, or adjusts is referred to as a "servicing operation." A servicing operation is performed when it is necessary either to modify the shape of a product or to restore it into a usable condition. An illustration of a servicing operation might be cleaning a spark plug or repairing a leak in a tire. These types of operations are performed in occupations like motor mechanics and fitting trades.

Designating an Operation

It is customary to express an operation with an introductory phrase—"how to." Here are a few examples:

1. How to drill a hole
2. How to rivet a joint
3. How to repair a leak in a tire

Sometimes *how* is eliminated and the operation is expressed in the following way:

1. To drill a hole
2. To rivet a joint
3. To repair a leak in a tire

Some instructors prefer to state the operations as an action in progress:

1. Drilling a hole
2. Riveting a joint
3. Repairing a leak in a tire

The manner of designating the operation is unimportant. However, consistency in the use of one form or another is desirable.

Not to get confused, an operation deals either with making or servicing a product. An operation has a purpose of its own and provides a suitable unit of instruction.

Operation Analysis

Within each division or phase of an occupation, the jobs will be listed. Each job is then analyzed and broken into different operations. For example, let's choose an occupation like machinist.

1. Divisions or phases of the occupation
   a. Drilling machine
   b. Lathe
   c. Shaping machine
   d. Milling machine

2. Jobs under division b (lathe) include, among others:
   a. Making a tommy bar
   b. Making a milling machine arbor
   c. Making a bolt

3. Operations under job c (making a bolt) include:
   a. Cutting the bar
   b. Mounting the bar on the lathe
   c. Turning the bar
   d. Cutting the thread
   e. Parting off

For administrative purpose, analysis may stop at the operation. But for instructional purposes, an operation will be further analyzed and broken down into steps. This helps to facilitate easy instruction. For example, let's break down the operation "cutting the bar" into steps:

1. Choose the right size bar (either hexagonal or round).
2. Measure the required length.
3. Hold the bar (either on the machine or in the vice).
4. Choose the correct blade.
5. Fix the blade on the frame.
6. Start cutting.

Some specific precautions should be observed while performing each operation. For the operation we have just discussed, the precautions will include:

1. using full length of the blade,
2. making sure to choose the correct blade for the material, and
3. cutting outside the marked line.

This should be done for all the involved operations in the course. For easy instruction and for reference purposes, an *operation sheet* should be drawn up for each operation. An operation sheet only tells the *how* of the operation and serves as a directive for the trainees. It also helps the trainees to go at their own pace.

An operation sheet contains the following:

1. Operation sheet number
2. Title of the operation
3. Description of the operation (in about a paragraph)
4. Description in steps of how the operation is to be carried out (each step should include specific precautions to be observed)
5. Illustrations of various operation steps (when necessary only)

Many instructors don't like to do the full operation analysis, especially those who don't have teaching qualifications. This is probably because they don't know how to go about the analysis. Or perhaps they think they have all phases of their course clear in their minds. However, they fail to realize that 50 percent of good teaching is careful planning.

Instructors should realize that their analysis should not be allowed to become static. They should keep abreast of new developments in their areas of specialty and introduce new information and techniques in their teaching, as well as drop obsolete practices.

It is important for the instructor to thoroughly understand what he or she must teach. Instructors are responsible for teaching and actual occupational techniques that are current practice. Real tools, equipment, materials, machinery, and practices must be used. Teachers in technical training do not simply tell trainees about jobs; they require their students to do the jobs.

Teachers of technical training must play various roles. The many functions include showing the way, clarifying a principle, explaining an operation, and interpreting written material. In order to do these things well, the teacher must understand the many skills required of him or her as an expert in his or her specialty.

There are, however, some considerations that will influence operation analysis. These include the age of the learner, the safety of the tools and machinery, the sequence according to the psychology of learning, physical limitations of the workshop, and opportunity of advancement within the organization and in the community.

Of importance is that instructors must

1. develop and clearly follow understood aims and objectives of the course,
2. recognize what trainees should learn (as indicated by the analysis), and
3. know and understand fully the implications of several principles of teaching that apply to organization.

Furthermore, the shop should not become a repair department for doing jobs—places with questionable educational value.

5

KNOWLEDGE CONTENT IN TECHNICAL TRAINING

Apart from the acquisition of skills, technical training should give trainees some knowledge about their job. This we call *related information*.

The information that is associated with technical training is classified as general, technical, socioeconomic, safety-related, and occupational.

General Information

General information is desirable for a trainee to know but not directly connected with any phase of the manipulative work. It is material that gives the trainee an understanding of some of the significant relationships of their instructional areas with occupational developments. This information is usually concerned with the manufacture of materials, invention of tools and machines, production methods, and industrial organization.

Here are a few examples of general information topics for our example topic:

1. Manufacture of iron and steel
2. Origin of the lathe
3. Development of the production system of manufacturing
4. How modern industry operates

Technical Information

Technical information includes material that helps a trainee form correct judgments and make proper decisions in performing the jobs or operations. It deals with specification of materials, fabricating procedures, tools, and machines.

The following are a few examples of technical information topics:

1. Fits, limits, and tolerances
2. Designing projects
3. Types of files
4. Taps and dies

Socioeconomic Information

Socioeconomic information helps a trainee understands how industry functions in the world in which people live and work. Such information is given less attention than is warranted. This is regrettable because the complexity of industry today requires all workers to have a much greater knowledge of socioeconomic issues than at any previous time in history.

Examples of topics concerned with the socioeconomic aspects of industry are

1. workmen's compensation,
2. trade unions,
3. social security,
4. quality and quantity production and cost, and
5. labor laws.

Safety Information

Safety information covers safety practices in the home and workshop. The need for stressing this type of information while at work is apparent, as industry places a great premium on safety.

Safety information should not be confused with the specific precautions that must be taught while demonstrating operations:

In addition to these safety practices, there are general safety topics that trainees should be given an opportunity to discuss.

Here are a few such safety information topics:

1. First aid
2. Importance of safety in the workshop
3. What the industry thinks of safety

Occupational Information

Occupational information guides the selection of and preparation for an occupation. It also includes such topics as how to keep a job, employment opportunities, compensation, and so on. It is especially good information in trade schools and apprenticeship training. The following examples show the nature of occupational information topics:

1. Working conditions and compensation
2. Preparation required for securing a job
3. Opportunities for advancement
4. Employee-employer relationship

Let's examine these topics in the framework of a specific occupation, say welding.

Two of the types information classified in this chapter are very necessary in technical training—technical information and safety information. These categories of information contribute to the mastery of the manipulative work while giving the trainee an important awareness about safety, both at home and at work.

The order in which this information should be given depends on the job, but most of it should be given twice and preferably on the job.

The extent to which the information should be given depends on the grade of training. For example, trainees participating in higher technical training should be given more information. Preferably, they should cover most or even all the classified information pertaining to their specialty. Those trainees at the lower grade, on the other hand, mostly require only the topics that will help them master their job.

Some of the categories of information should be covered formally, and others are better addressed informally. Informal imparting of knowledge takes place during the course of the instructor's daily contacts with trainees and should be given in relation to matters as they arise; either from trainees' difficulties or from their questions.

The imparting of this type of knowledge should be formal only in the sense of following a prescribed pattern and plan; the actual sharing can be done in informal talks and short lectures. A program should be drawn up and fit into the timetable in such a way that it breaks up the work on the operation and provides variety and rest from physical activity.

Related information should not be confused with the term *related subjects*. When organized courses, such as those on drawing, mathematics, and sciences are taught as separate courses, they are generally known as *related subjects*. Related information, on the other hand, is taught by the instructor as an essential part of his or her course. Related subjects are often identified with federally reimbursed classes—that is to say, related subjects are more pronounced in trade and technical schools.

General information topics should not be considered as incidental instructional material. They should carry the same status in a course as the operations. Since they have their own identity, related information topics should be taught as separate lessons.

6

PLANNING THE TRAINING WORKSHOP

Given that the training workshop is an instructional area where technical trainees will spend most of their time, careful planning is necessary. It's important to avoid bottlenecks, waste of materials, accidents at work, waste of instructor's and trainees' time, and bad housekeeping. The shop should also be planned to contain modern amenities, as this is a source of motivation for the trainees. And moreover, provision should be made for future extension.

At the initial stage of the planning, it is necessary to follow these procedures:

1. Write down the objectives of the workshop.
2. Consider the financial standing of the organization.
3. Determine the capacity of the shop at a given time—in other words, the maximum number of trainees the shop will serve at a time.
4. Determine the location of the shop.
5. Determine the equipment needed for the training.
6. Prepare the layout of the shop.
7. Consider the storage facilities.
8. Consider safety in and around the shop.

To make the planning a comprehensive one, the training officer should ask questions from those with experience in the same line, manufacturers, the organization that owns the shop, and the community in which the workshop is going to be situated.

Workshop Objectives

Before considering the workshop objectives, the organization's objectives and policies relating to training must be clear and kept in mind. This will avoid unnecessary changes and complications. The workshop objectives themselves should specify whether the shop is meant for apprenticeship training or for retraining programs alone. In addition, they should note which trade or trades it would serve. It should further state the level of training and duration of the training program. This statement of objectives will help determine what tools and equipment are necessary.

Financial Standing

The financial standing of the organization will specify the amount budgeted for the establishment of the training department and subsequent grants that will be allocated to the department annually. In light of this information, the training officer will be able to determine the shop's capacity and will also be able to modify the workshop objectives if need be. Equipment choices, including size, may also be determined by the organization's financial standing.

Capacity of the Shop

The capacity of the shop is the maximum number of trainees the shop will cater to at a time. This can be determined from availability of funds, the length of the course, staff availability, policies of the organization, and the local bylaws.

A technical training class usually has a maximum of fifteen trainees. This enables good supervision and thorough instruction. The need is, however, the governing factor in determining the size of a class.

Location of the Shop

Before the site of the training workshop can be determined, the training officer will have to know the extent to which the community needs the trainees after graduation. In addition, a study of the local bylaws is important. The trainer must also take into consideration the conditions prevailing at the time and the safety of trainees and the staff.

If the workshop is for a company, it is suggested that the shop be built near the company's largest factory. If it is a group training workshop, having the center central to all the factories should be considered. Or perhaps one of the factories will require the most training, in which case proximity to that facility should be prioritized.

On the other hand, if the workshop is for the government, the location will have to be in a community where the graduates of the shop will be easily employed and where the training equipment could be easily obtained or transported.

The workshop planner should bear in mind that

1. the workshop should be established in a location that enables ease of transportation of equipment and training personal;
2. the workshop should not be located where there would a possibility of danger to the trainees—for example an earthquake or an explosion; and
3. the shop should not be far from the room where academic courses will be taught.

Equipment Consideration

Before the shop plan can be made, all machines, workbenches, and materials needed for the training must be listed so as to plan for their installation and storage.

The choice of machines and equipment size can be determined based on trainees' needs. For example, if the shop is in a vestibule school, the smallest of the machines being used in the factory should be purchased. Or if there is a surplus of certain machines in the factory, they can be transported to the workshop. On the other hand, if the shop is meant for apprenticeship training only, it's important to purchase the machines that would serve the purpose of giving the basic skills necessary for the trade. In such a case, mass production machines should be avoided. New developments on the machines that will be used for retraining should be incorporated immediately upon their introduction.

It is suggested that a maximum of one meter should be allowed around each machine and on the working side of the bench. However, great consideration must be given to safety.

Layout of the Shop

The usual practice in determining the size of a training workshop is to go by the maximum number of trainees the workshop will serve at a given time. The minimum area allocated to a trainee in technical training is five square meters. If a workshop will serve a total of fifteen trainees at a time, the minimum area of the shop, the equation $5 \times 15 = 75$ shows that the shop should be at least seventy-five square meters. This includes the instructor's office and the stores.

The maximum ratio of width to length of a workshop is usually one to two and a minimum of one to one-half. The minimum width of a shop is usually ten meters, but the wider the width, the more natural light comes in—which is what is required.

The next step after determining the shop's size is making the plan. In making the plan, the following steps should be taken:

1. Create rough sketches made to scale on graph paper to locate the positions of the machines, benches, cabinets, tool storage, material storage, and finishing room.
2. Use paper templates representing to scale the various pieces of equipment. Moving the placement of the equipment about on the sketch can help to determine final locations.
3. Next, prepare a floor plan from the sketch.
4. Indicate all outlets needed for air, gas, and water. Locate washbowls and other sanitary features.
5. Locate chalkboards, display boards, and racks for stock.

When making the plan, however, it is good to keep the following in mind:

- The classroom and instructor's office should be on the north side of the shop—to avoid sunshine.
- Window space, as a general rule, should not be less than one-fourth of the floor space.

- Shops should have at least two exits, one of which should be wide enough (a minimum of three meters) to permit moving large equipment in or out.
- All parts of the shop must be visible to the teacher.
- A display area should be located near the entrance to the shop
- The instructor's office should be made with a glass partition.
- A cloakroom should be located near the entrance to the workshop.
- The ceiling of the shop should be at least four meters high, or possibly there should be no ceiling at all.
- Partitions in the shop should be movable.
- Concrete floors are good where heavy machinery will be used.
- The classroom walls should be made with acoustical material.
- Project planning areas should be in the center of the shop.
- Fluorescent light should be used in the shop, but the more natural light the better.
- Material and tool stores should be located within the shop or centrally located.

Storage Facilities

The training shop requires two main storage areas—one for tools and another for materials. In case of apprenticeship training, a third area may be needed for the display of projects.

Tools Storage

In the workshop, there are usually general tools and personal tools.

General tools are the tools that every trainee can use and are not frequently used. They are usually kept in a tool crib or tool panel. A tool crib is a tool storage cutout within the workshop for keeping tools. It requires a storekeeper who issues and receives tools from the trainees.

The storekeeper is usually appointed on a weekly basis from among the trainees. This is especially common in apprenticeship training. Tool panels are commonly used nowadays both in trade schools and industries because they

1. save space,
2. make for easy access to the tools,
3. make for easy checking of the tools, and
4. allow for a good display of tools.

Personal tools or tools that are frequently used are issued to the trainees and are kept in a tool kit or toolbox. The trainees can carry the box to their workbenches or any place they are going to practice. Having personal tools gives the trainees the responsibility of keeping their tools.

Other facilities for tool storage include the following:

1. Tool cabinets. Cabinets accommodate light or heavy tools and are used where a limited number of tools are needed for the operation of the shop and in specialized shops.
2. Movable tool racks. Movable racks are used where heavy tools need to be stored—such as in heavy equipment repair shops. The rack can easily be moved to work stations.

With a well-planned and operated series of tool storage facilities, the trainees can learn

1. the correct names of tools,
2. maintenance of tools,
3. methods of mounting tools,
4. issuing of tools,
5. cost of tools,
6. use of tool catalogues, and
7. proper use of tools.

Material Storage

Materials such as metal bars or plywood should be stored on vertical racks because they take up less space than horizontal racks. Ceiling height is a factor that must be considered in vertical storage of bars. When a vertical rack is used, the base should be pitched slightly to prevent boards from falling forward into the room. Slanting the base will also permit the available space behind the rack to be used for the storage of panels. Some people, however, prefer to use horizontal racks. In this case, the rack must be well fastened to the wall. These materials should be stored near the sawing machine or the vices. There should be a wide passageway (enough for a truck) to the materials rack for easy supply and removal.

For other types of materials, consider

1. a wall-type storage rack for bar clamps, C-clamps, and hand screws placed next to the assembly area;
2. supply cabinets for nails, emery cloth, and so on below tool panels or adjacent to the panel; and
3. steel cabinets for storage of all paint, stain, oil, grease, and other volatile materials.

All heavy tools or materials must be stored at the bottom of the rack.

There should be a "running inventory" system, which ensures periodic attention to shortage and, at the same time, gives trainees an opportunity to assume responsibilities.

Project Storage

Consider the following when planning project storage units so as to avoid confusion, inferior finished projects, and general discouragement:

1. Plan for individual storage units in the general storeroom if possible.
2. Provide some free storage floor area within the storage room for unfinished but assembled projects that may be too large for regular storage lockers or cubicles.
3. Plan for finished project display through the use of built-in and well-lit display cases facing corridors. If possible, provide walk-in access to the display cases.

The general and localized storage provisions for tools, materials, and projects for any shop program can only prove satisfactory if due thought has been given to the need for flexibility, efficiency, and safety.

Safety

All this effort of planning and arranging the workshop will be defeated if the trainees cannot work there safely.

Three areas are to be considered in making a workshop a safe place to work:

1. Mechanical aspects
2. Color aspects
3. Housekeeping

Mechanical

1. All the machines that are to be used must be guarded.
2. Good ventilating, good lighting, and so forth must be provided.
3. There must be a grounding system for all electrical equipment.
4. All hand tools must be in a good condition for work.
5. One or more fire extinguishers must be provided, especially very near where volatile materials are kept.

Color

1. Dangerous parts of machines must be marked with a special color (red).
2. Danger zones must be blocked off with paint (cream white).
3. All control handles, nubs, and so forth that are handled for operation should be painted yellow.
4. The base and other parts of the machines are to be painted green.

The advantages of using scientifically arranged color schemes include the following:

1. Improvement of trainees' morale
2. Reduction of fatigue
3. Addition of beauty to the shop
4. Reduction of accidents

Housekeeping

1. Provisions must be made for dust collection.
2. Utilities must be conveyed by providing dustbins.
3. The aisles must be rid of scraps, oils, and so forth. Provide a scrap box and other appropriate bins for the discarding of materials.
4. Safety posters should be fixed near the machines and neatly around the shop.

There is no single or specific answer to the question of how one achieves an ideal workshop. Safety, economy, and good appearance are just the guiding factors.

ABOUT THE AUTHOR

Adebayo Ojo is a Canadian qualified engineer and a registered vocational teacher in the province of New Brunswick.

He has consulted and assisted in establishing many vocational and industrial training centers across Africa and other countries.

He is also a chartered specialist plant and equipment valuer and was a partner in Knight Frank Nigeria.

ABOUT THE BOOK

Modern Methods of Vocational and Industrial Training is a handbook for vocational and industrial training specialists.

With rapid developments in science and information technology, modern methods of training in skills acquisition and industrial training are necessary. New tools and labor reductions in the manufacturing and services industries are the order of the day. Old methods of skills acquisition must be dropped in order to meet the rapid industrial and commercial developments.

Modern Methods, presented in six chapters, explores a systematic approach to carrying out skills acquisition and retraining to meet the demands of a new industrial age.

Printed in the United States
By Bookmasters